Saving Our World

WATER
POLLUTION

Sean Price

mc **Marshall Cavendish**
Benchmark

New York

Marshall Cavendish Benchmark
99 White Plains Road
Tarrytown, NY 10591
www.marshallcavendish.us

Library of Congress Cataloging-in-Publication Data
Price, Sean.
    Water pollution / By Sean Price.
    p. cm. -- (Saving our world)
    Includes bibliographical references and index.
    ISBN 978-0-7614-3221-0
  1. Water--Pollution--Juvenile literature. I. Title.
    TD422.P75 2008
    363.739'4--dc22
    2008014552

The photographs in this book are used by permission and through the courtesy of:

Half Title: Dejan Lazarevic / Shutterstock
Vankina / Shutterstock: 4-5, Bennett Productions / Oxford Scientific (OSF) / Photolibrary,
Associated Press: 8-9, Lane Erickson / Dreamstime: 10-11, Don Mason / Flirt Collection /
Photolibrary: 12-13, Pawel Kanicki / Picture Press / Photolibrary: 14-15,
The Print Collector / Imagestate RM / Photolibrary: 16, Associated Press: 17, Dejan Lazarevic
/ Shutterstock: 18-19, Associated Press: 18b, Marcokopp / Istockphoto: 20-21,
Howard Hall / Oxford Scientific (OSF) / Photolibrary: 22, Dave Fleetham / Pacific Stock
/ Photolibray: 23, Associated Press: 24-25, Alistair Scott / Shutterstock: 26-27, Corbis /
Jupiterimages: 28-29.
Cover photo: David Woodfall / Gettyimages; Brasil2/Istockphoto; PaulPaladin /
Shutterstock; Oleg Prikhodko/Istockphoto.
Illustrations: Q2AMedia Art Bank
Created by: Q2A Media
Creative Director: Simmi Sikka
Series Editor: Maura Christopher
Series Art Director: Sudakshina Basu
Series Designers: Dibakar Acharjee, Joita Das, Mansi Mittal, Rati Mathur and Shruti Bahl
Series Illustrator: Abhideep Jha and Ajay Sharma
Photo research by Sejal Sehgal
Series Project Managers: Ravneet Kaur and Shekhar Kapur
Printed in Malaysia

1 3 5 6 4 2

CONTENTS

Polluted Water

Take a long, cool drink of water. Then imagine seeing tiny bits of garbage floating in your glass. Now you understand why water pollution is so serious.

How Do People Pollute?

Water becomes polluted when something dangerous is added to it. That something might be trash, sewage, or a chemical. When people drink, bathe, or swim in polluted water, the pollution can make them sick. It can even kill them. Polluted water is also dangerous to animals and plants. Fish and frogs cannot thrive in polluted water. Land animals such as raccoons and bears cannot safely drink it.

What's in the Water?

Many substances can pollute water. Human waste is one of the biggest sources of pollution. Every day, 2 million tons of human waste gets dumped into water worldwide. Factories produce chemicals that get dumped into waterways as well. Chemicals used on farms and lawns also pollute. Rain washes those chemicals into lakes, rivers, and streams.

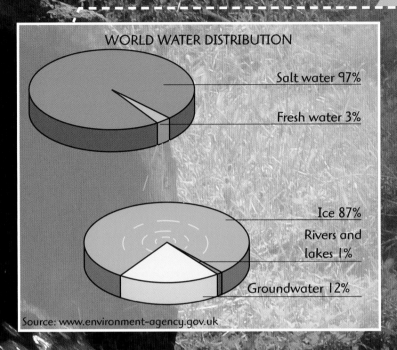

WORLD WATER DISTRIBUTION

Salt water 97%

Fresh water 3%

Ice 87%

Rivers and lakes 1%

Groundwater 12%

Source: www.environment-agency.gov.uk

A Watery Planet
Two-thirds of the Earth is covered with water. But 97 percent of that water is in the Earth's oceans. Of the fresh water that's left, 87 percent is ice. It is found in the form of glaciers, giant ice sheets, and on snowy mountain tops. Less than one percent of the Earth's water can be used for drinking, cooking, and bathing.

Some types of water pollution are natural, such as too much dirt washing into a stream. These natural types of pollution usually wash away quickly. However, humanmade types of pollution tend to remain. They can destroy much of the wildlife in an area.

Getting to the Point

Water pollution can be broken down into two main types. These are point and nonpoint pollution.

Point Pollution

Point pollution has a point of origin, or a source, that is easy to find. Ships carrying oil sometimes leak. This creates a big patch of oil in the water called an **oil slick**. The point of origin for that oil slick is easy to spot. It's the ship! The same would be true of a factory dumping chemicals in a lake. Point pollution is the easiest to identify. That means it's also the easiest to stop.

QUESTION TIME

What is groundwater?

Groundwater collects in the cracks and spaces underground. Some of those spaces are very large. Large underground pools of water are called **aquifers**. Groundwater from wells and aquifers supplies drinking water to about half the United States. Groundwater also supplies water to many lakes, ponds, and streams.

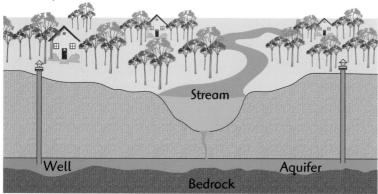

Nonpoint Pollution

Nonpoint pollution sources are scattered around in different places. Nonpoint pollution might come from a parking lot where a car has leaked oil. Or, it might come from a golf course that uses chemicals called **fertilizers** to make plants grow. The oil and fertilizers—dangerous liquids—seep into the ground. They mix with rainwater or melted snow and collect in nearby waterways. Pollution from nonpoint sources is difficult to spot. That makes this type of pollution harder to stop.

This ship is leaking oil. The lighter patches of water show where the oil slick has formed. An oil slick can do great damage to ocean wildlife. The oil coats plants and animals in a sticky layer of black slime. The oil makes it hard for living creatures to breathe or move. Sadly, plants and animals caught in oil slicks will die.

Sewage

Sewage is the material we throw away in our drains and sewers. It includes all kinds of trash and garbage, as well as human waste.

The History of Garbage

People have dumped garbage in the water since prehistoric times. In the past 200 years or so, this has become a big problem. In earlier times, most trash was made of natural materials such as food scraps, wood, cloth, or clay. These items were **biodegradable**. That means they broke down, or decomposed, naturally. But many modern items, including plastic bottles and bags, do not break down easily.

Down the Drain

Human and animal waste is a common type of water pollution. This type of **sewage** has always been dumped into rivers, lakes, and oceans. But the world's population has grown sharply in the past 200 years. In 1800, about 200,000 people lived in a typical big city. Today, the world's biggest cities average about 6.2 million people. So the amount of waste they produce has grown rapidly. Most rivers and lakes near big cities are now too polluted to go swimming in or to fish in.

Most sewers consists of pipes under the ground. These pipes take waste away from people's toilets and sinks. Few people think about where their sewage winds up.

EYE-OPENER

Drugs in the Water

Pollution can take unexpected forms. People swallow billions of pills each year to fight illnesses. Farm animals are also fed drugs, including **antibiotics**, to make them grow and keep them healthy. Small amounts of those drugs turn up in human and animal waste. That sewage ends up in the water. Scientists are still not sure how much pollution from drugs affects humans. But it has been shown to sicken or kill some plants.

Industrial Pollution

Every year factories worldwide create at least 300 million tons of pollutants. Much of that pollution winds up in our water. But laws have limited this type of pollution.

A Humanmade Problem

Industrial pollution includes many different types of humanmade products. Much of the pollution comes from chemicals such as PCBs, which are used in plastics and car products. Highly poisonous metals, such as mercury and lead, are also used in mining and manufacturing. Small amounts of these metals get into the wastewater of mines and factories. They wind up in our water systems. These chemicals and metals do not break down quickly. Accidentally drinking even small amounts of them can harm someone's health. For instance, mercury harms nerves and causes brain damage. Many chemicals cause cancer.

Much of the acid rain in the United States comes from electric power plants that burn coal. Another big cause of acid rain is exhaust from cars and trucks.

Why does the sky always look clearer after a good rain?

When it rains, small bits of pollution in the air are caught on the way down. The rain brings this air pollution down to Earth. The chemicals in that air pollution boost the acid content in the rainwater. They create **acid rain**. Acid rain can kill or weaken plants, fish, and wild animals.

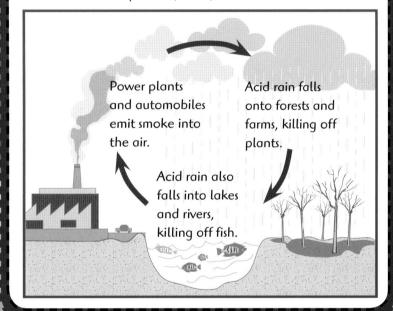

Power plants and automobiles emit smoke into the air.

Acid rain falls onto forests and farms, killing off plants.

Acid rain also falls into lakes and rivers, killing off fish.

Clean Water Act

In 1972 the United States passed a law called the **Clean Water Act**. It helped clean up factories and other sources of point pollution. Today, more than 75 percent of chemicals are removed from factory water before it can be released into rivers and lakes. However, nonpoint pollution remains a serious problem. Chemicals from nonpoint sources include **pesticides** (insect killers) used in yards and on golf courses. About 40 percent of all U.S. rivers and lakes are not clean enough for fishing or swimming, due to nonpoint pollution.

Down on the Farm

Two types of pollutants that come from farms are animal waste and chemicals. Pollution from farms greatly harms U.S. rivers and lakes.

Crop dusting airplanes like this one spread chemicals on farm fields. They help plants grow and protect them from insects. Most chemicals wash off the plants. But they seep into nearby lakes and streams. Consuming these chemicals can hurt people and animals.

Fertilizers and Pesticides

One farm can use tons of fertilizers to help its crops grow. Farms also use a lot of pesticides, and tractors spill oil and gas. Meanwhile, plowing the ground for crops loosens the dirt. Rain washes away the chemicals, oil, and dirt into nearby lakes and rivers. This polluted water also seeps into aquifers. As a result, the water becomes poisoned.

Fertilizers help plants to grow. When these chemicals wash into water, they help algae to grow faster and die faster. Both of these processes take oxygen out of the water. In some cases, it robs the water of all its oxygen. This process is called **eutrophication**. As a result, fish and plants cannot live in those areas. Thanks to eutrophication, wildlife cannot live in much of the Mississippi River. More than half of all U.S. farmland drains into that river.

A Smelly Problem

Farms produce a lot of animal waste. North Carolina's 10 million hogs produce twice as much urine and solid waste as people in Los Angeles, New York, and Chicago. Many farms have waste lagoons—big pits full of animal waste. These lagoons are supposed to be lined with plastic. But rocks and sticks often puncture the plastic. Lagoons can also overflow during rainstorms. That can release tons of smelly animal waste into nearby waterways. This can kill the wildlife that live in the water or that drink it.

Getting Treatment

Some water in the United States is seriously polluted. Still, Americans have some of the cleanest drinking water in the world. That is because cities often treat, or clean up, the water people drink.

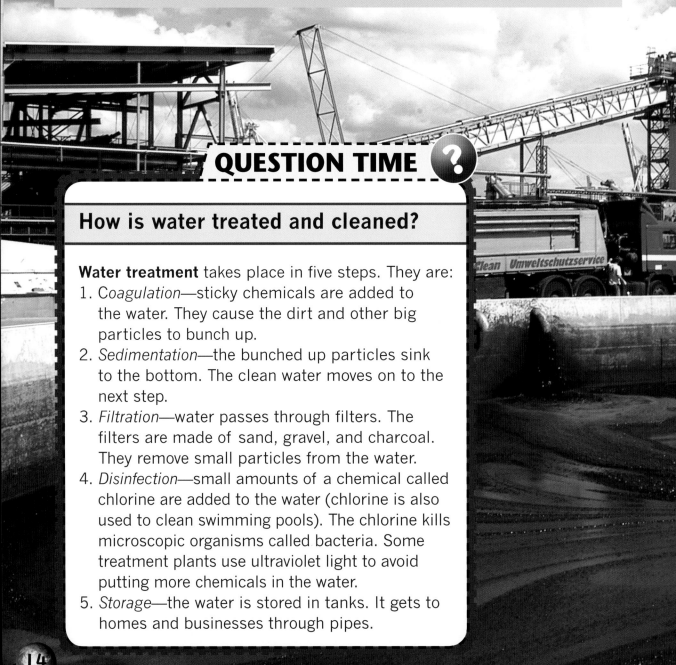

QUESTION TIME ?

How is water treated and cleaned?

Water treatment takes place in five steps. They are:

1. *Coagulation*—sticky chemicals are added to the water. They cause the dirt and other big particles to bunch up.
2. *Sedimentation*—the bunched up particles sink to the bottom. The clean water moves on to the next step.
3. *Filtration*—water passes through filters. The filters are made of sand, gravel, and charcoal. They remove small particles from the water.
4. *Disinfection*—small amounts of a chemical called chlorine are added to the water (chlorine is also used to clean swimming pools). The chlorine kills microscopic organisms called bacteria. Some treatment plants use ultraviolet light to avoid putting more chemicals in the water.
5. *Storage*—the water is stored in tanks. It gets to homes and businesses through pipes.

Making the Return Trip

Water that is flushed down toilets is **wastewater**. So is the water that goes down sinks. This water is treated before it is put back into rivers and lakes, which helps reduce pollution. The treatment process for wastewater is much the same as for drinking water. However, some homes and businesses do not follow laws for disposing of wastewater. This means sewage from one million U.S. homes still enters the environment untreated.

Many countries do not treat their wastewater at all. One out of every six people lives without access to safe drinking water, according to a United Nations report.

Troubled Waters

Polluted water can cause diseases. These diseases have killed millions of people throughout history.

The Time of Cholera

In the mid-1800s people in the Wild West feared outlaws and Indians. But they feared a disease called **cholera** even more. People with cholera suffered terrible diarrhea and vomiting. Nobody understood how cholera spread. Finally, in 1854, a doctor named John Snow found that it was caused by drinking water that was polluted with human waste. Cholera killed hundreds of thousands of people in the United States and Europe. It has killed millions worldwide.

Father Thames shows his offspring—Diphtheria, Scrofura, and Cholera—to London, represented by the woman on the left. Diphtheria, Scrofula, and Cholera are all diseases caused by polluted water that plagued London in the 1850s.

EYE-OPENER

Water-treatment plants make water-borne illnesses rare in the United States. But old pipes and outdated treatment centers can fail to clean water of deadly germs. One study found that seven million Americans become sick each year from contaminated tap water.

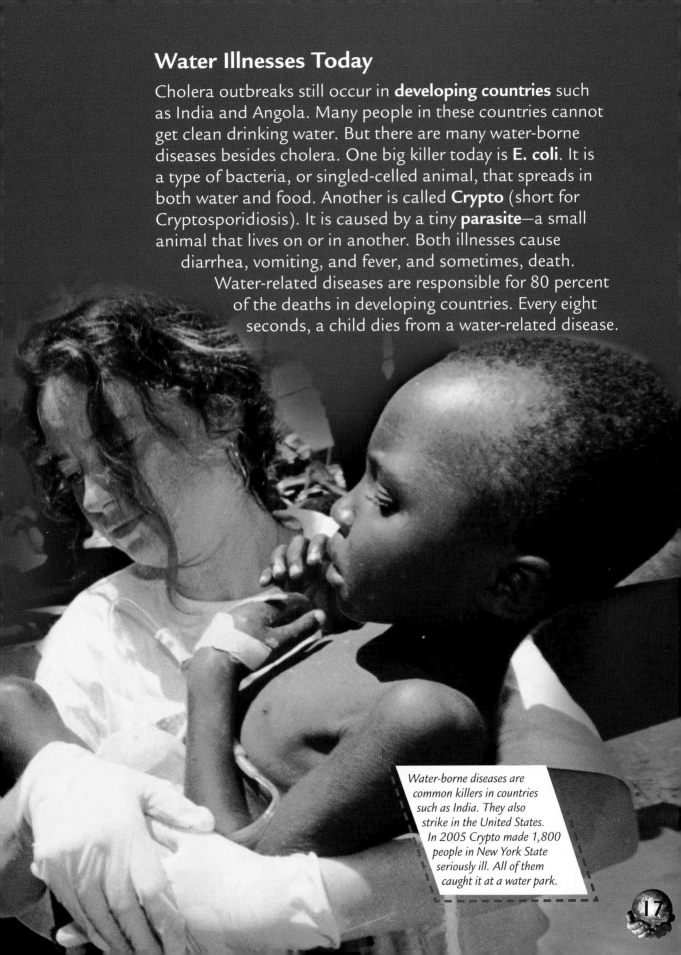

Water Illnesses Today

Cholera outbreaks still occur in **developing countries** such as India and Angola. Many people in these countries cannot get clean drinking water. But there are many water-borne diseases besides cholera. One big killer today is **E. coli**. It is a type of bacteria, or singled-celled animal, that spreads in both water and food. Another is called **Crypto** (short for Cryptosporidiosis). It is caused by a tiny **parasite**—a small animal that lives on or in another. Both illnesses cause diarrhea, vomiting, and fever, and sometimes, death. Water-related diseases are responsible for 80 percent of the deaths in developing countries. Every eight seconds, a child dies from a water-related disease.

Water-borne diseases are common killers in countries such as India. They also strike in the United States. In 2005 Crypto made 1,800 people in New York State seriously ill. All of them caught it at a water park.

17

More Troubled Waters

In 1969 the Cuyahoga River burst into flames. It wasn't the first time river in Cleveland, Ohio, had caught fire. At least nine other fires had started there because of chemicals and trash polluting the river.

A Dead River

The Cuyahoga River had been used as a sewer for decades. Companies dumped tons of chemicals and trash in it each year. People in Cleveland had a joke about the river. They said anyone who fell into the Cuyahoga did not drown, they decayed. Fish and wildlife could not live in the Cuyahoga. The river flowed into Lake Erie, one of the Great Lakes. This pollution helped kill off almost all the fish and plants in Lake Erie.

New laws caused companies to stop dumping chemicals in the Cuyahoga and other rivers. It also forced them to treat sewage before releasing it into rivers and lakes. Pollution remains a problem on troubled rivers like the Cuyahoga. But many parts of the river are now so clean that people can catch fish.

Tough U.S. laws have helped clean up many waterways, like the Cuyahoga. But pollution remains a problem in many places. Many countries still treat rivers and lakes as dumps for trash and sewage.

Why is the 1969 Cuyahoga River fire important?

The Cuyahoga River fire caught national attention in 1969. It led to the founding of the **Environmental Protection Agency** (EPA) in 1970. The EPA is the governmental body that fights pollution. The river fire also spurred the creation of laws that stop water pollution. The most important of these were the Clean Water Act of 1972 and the **Safe Drinking Water Act** of 1974. These and other laws forced companies and people to clean up the Cuyahoga and other rivers. Today, almost seventy types of fish live in the once **dead zone** areas near Cleveland.

Saving the Bald Eagle

In 1970 water pollution was killing the bald eagle. Americans were shocked to find that their national symbol might die out.

Bad Eggs

The main problem was a pesticide called **DDT**. Most farms used DDT. Rain and snow washed the chemical into rivers and lakes. Fish drank water that contained DDT, but it did not kill them. Instead, it built up in their bodies. When bald eagles ate the fish, the DDT built up in their bodies as well. The DDT caused eagles to lay eggs with very thin shells. Mother eagles who sat on these eggs accidentally cracked them and killed their young.

DDT harmed bald eagles. It made it difficult for eagles to hatch eggs. People did not realize it, but DDT hurt humans in much the same way. It damaged nerves and made it difficult for women to have babies. DDT is now banned in the United States, but it is still legal in some other countries.

Banning DDT

For many years, the bald eagle was listed by the U.S. government as an **endangered species**. That meant all bald eagles were in danger of dying out. In 1963 there were only 417 pairs of bald eagles left in the lower forty-eight states. Laws created in the 1970s banned DDT. By 1995 there were 4,712 pairs of eagles. That meant the eagle was no longer an endangered species. Today, eagles are thriving, thanks to greater awareness about water pollution.

EYE-OPENER

Writer Rachel Carson's book *Silent Spring* helped save the bald eagles. The book was published in 1962. It showed how pesticides such as DDT hurt the environment. *Silent Spring* quickly became a best seller. Carson's book raised public awareness about all types of pollution. It is given credit for starting the environmental movement.

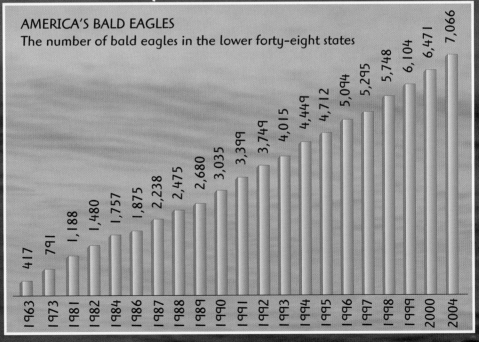

AMERICA'S BALD EAGLES
The number of bald eagles in the lower forty-eight states

Year	Number
1963	417
1973	791
1981	1,188
1982	1,480
1984	1,757
1986	1,875
1987	2,238
1988	2,475
1989	2,680
1990	3,035
1991	3,399
1992	3,749
1993	4,015
1994	4,449
1995	4,712
1996	5,094
1997	5,295
1998	5,748
1999	6,104
2000	6,471
2004	7,066

Note: Data ends in 2004 because many states stopped conducting annual surveys after the bald eagle population significantly increased.

Climate Change

The Earth's temperature is rising. Some experts predict it will warm by about 3.2 degrees Fahrenheit (1.8 degrees Celsius) this century. This heat is harming the world's oceans.

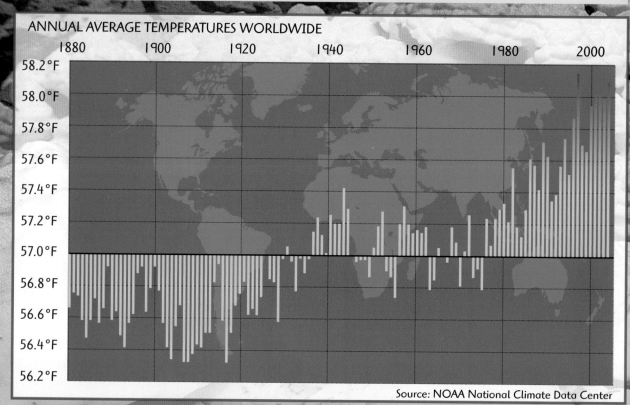

ANNUAL AVERAGE TEMPERATURES WORLDWIDE

Source: NOAA National Climate Data Center

Temperatures have been rising worldwide since 1880. The yellow bars on this chart show Earth's average yearly temperature. Before the 1930s, those temperatures averaged below 57° F. Since then, they have averaged several degrees above 57° F. That is enough to radically change the earth's climate.

Ocean Life in Danger

A temperature rise of 3.2 degrees Fahrenheit (1.8 degrees Celsius) may not sound like much. But the top ten warmest years of the last century have all occurred since 1990. Human activity—especially the release of **greenhouse gases** from cars and factories—is blamed for this warming. Rising global temperatures cause **thermal** (heat) **pollution** in the world's oceans. Thermal pollution causes serious damage to coral reefs. Corals also need clean, clear water in order to thrive.

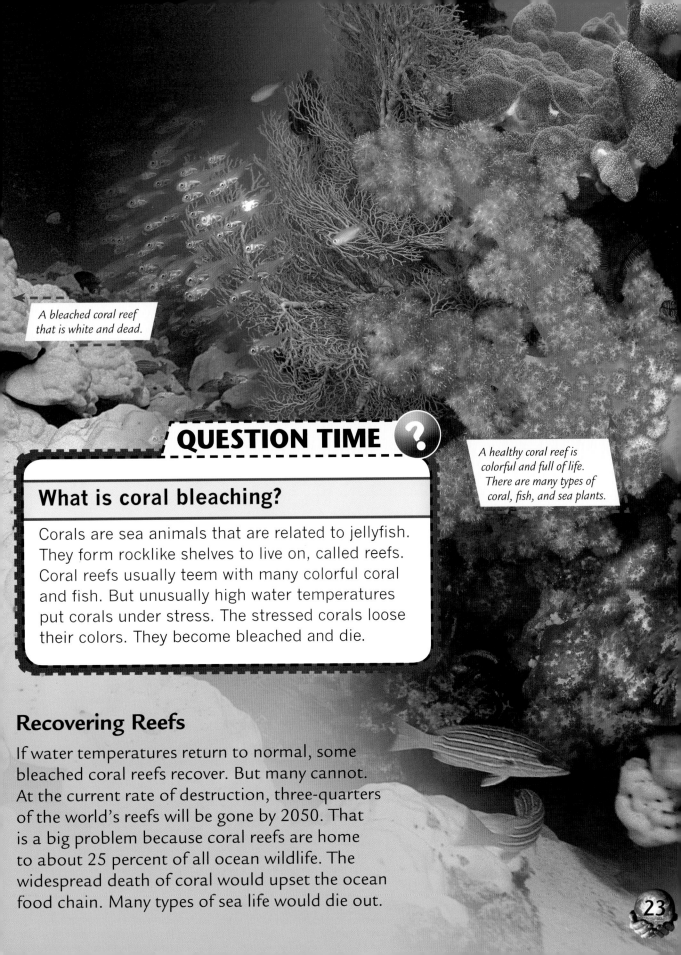

A bleached coral reef that is white and dead.

A healthy coral reef is colorful and full of life. There are many types of coral, fish, and sea plants.

QUESTION TIME ?

What is coral bleaching?

Corals are sea animals that are related to jellyfish. They form rocklike shelves to live on, called reefs. Coral reefs usually teem with many colorful coral and fish. But unusually high water temperatures put corals under stress. The stressed corals loose their colors. They become bleached and die.

Recovering Reefs

If water temperatures return to normal, some bleached coral reefs recover. But many cannot. At the current rate of destruction, three-quarters of the world's reefs will be gone by 2050. That is a big problem because coral reefs are home to about 25 percent of all ocean wildlife. The widespread death of coral would upset the ocean food chain. Many types of sea life would die out.

Water Heroes

People can fight for clean, unpolluted water in many ways.

One Adult Makes a Big Difference

Jean-Michel Cousteau grew up living on the oceans. His father was the explorer Jacques Cousteau. He helped invent scuba tanks and underwater cameras. Jean-Michel has carried on his father's efforts to educate people about the oceans. He has helped produce many television shows about the need to protect undersea life from pollution and other threats. He also speaks to thousands of students every year. In 2006 Cousteau helped convince President George W. Bush to set up the Northwest Hawaiian Islands Marine National Monument. It is the world's largest park dedicated to preserving sea life.

Kids Make a Difference, Too

In 2007 students at Fowler Middle School in Tigard, Oregon, had a problem. Water from the school's parking lot ran off into nearby Summer Creek. The parking lot water was full of oil, gasoline, and other car chemicals. These chemicals were polluting the creek. So the students created a plant-filled pond between the parking lot and the stream. The pond keeps the water from the parking lot from flowing straight into the creek. Meanwhile, the plants in the pond help soak up and block pollutants. That makes the creek water cleaner.

Jean-Michel Cousteau has dedicated himself to educating people about the oceans. He has even appeared on special DVD features about sea life for the movies like Finding Nemo and SpongeBob SquarePants: The Movie.

Stop Pollution

Here are a few important steps that kids can take to help stop water pollution.

Dispose of Chemicals Properly

Take old chemicals to **recycling** centers. You can also take them to local dumps that are equipped to handle hazardous wastes. Chemicals include common household items like old batteries, motor oil, and pesticides. Do not flush them down the toilet or dump them in the backyard. Also, do not throw them in the regular trash. That trash ends up in **landfills** (places to bury trash) where the chemicals can leak into the ground.

QUESTION TIME

What can kids do to conserve water?

Take short showers. Try to keep them under five minutes. Also, shut off the water while brushing your teeth. Fix leaky faucets and toilets. Don't water the yard for hours at a time. Remember that using hot water burns up energy, which produces greenhouse gases. Also, less wastewater means less energy is used at treatment plants.

HOW THE AVERAGE PERSON USES WATER INSIDE THE HOME

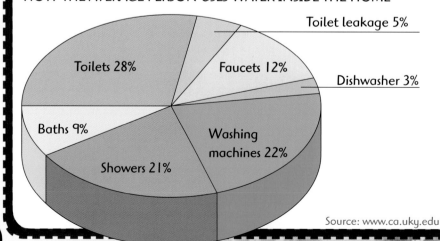

- Toilets 28%
- Faucets 12%
- Toilet leakage 5%
- Dishwasher 3%
- Washing machines 22%
- Showers 21%
- Baths 9%

Source: www.ca.uky.edu

Limit Use of Chemicals

Try to avoid using fertilizers and pesticides. Also, try to avoid using gasoline and oil for home appliances such as lawn mowers and snow blowers. These chemicals and **fossil fuels** seep into the ground and pollute water. There are some types of pesticide that are biodegradable. They break down quickly and become harmless to plants and animals. The soap and bleach used to clean dishes and laundry can also harm wildlife. Try to run full loads in the dishwasher or washing machine.

Cleaning up a mess is always tougher than preventing a mess. So take steps to prevent water pollution. Following these tips will save energy, which cuts down on air and water pollution. They also save time and money.

Kids Can Do More

Somewhere near you, there is a body of water that needs cleaning up. Can you meet the challenge of getting the job done?

Identify the Clean-up Site

Perhaps it is a lake or river with litter along its banks. Maybe it's a swamp or wetland that local people use as a dump. Perhaps it is a nearby beach that is choked with debris from the sea. If you don't know of a polluted waterway, do some research. Ask your parents, teacher, and friends. Go to the library and ask for local articles on the subject.

EYE-OPENER

Make it Fun

Most people don't want to give up a weekend day to work. So turn your event into a good time. See if a local company will make T-shirts in return for advertising their products during the clean-up. Buy pizza or make something tasty for those who help out. If you are cleaning up litter, hold a contest to see who finds the most interesting piece of garbage. Give a prize to the winner.

Figure Out How to Clean It Up

Talk to the people who own the place that you want to clean up. Tell them about your plan. Ask for advice about the best way to meet your goals. Talk to other experts as well. Check with local chapters of groups such as the Sierra Club.

28

Cleaning up a polluted waterway can be hard work. You will learn a lot about the carelessness that leads to pollution. But cleaning up pollution can be a fun way to meet people or spend time with friends. It is also very rewarding.

Glossary

acid rain: Water that contains a lot of acid-forming pollution.

antibiotic: Drug that can kill bacteria.

aquifer: Large underground pool of water.

biodegradable: Able to break down naturally.

cholera: A disease caused by using water polluted with human waste.

Clean Water Act: Law passed in 1972 that stopped major types of water pollution.

Crypto (Cryptosporidiosis): A water-borne illness that causes diarrhea, vomiting, and fever.

DDT: A pesticide that has been banned in the United States.

dead zone: Part of a waterway that is so polluted that it cannot support life.

developing country: A country that is poor but growing economically.

E. coli: A type of bacteria in food and water that can cause diarrhea, vomiting, and fever.

endangered species: A plant or animal that could die out completely without protection.

Environmental Protection Agency (EPA): The U.S. agency that fights pollution.

eutrophication: Process that consumes the oxygen in water.

fossil fuel: Coal, oil, or natural gas made from the remains of former life.

fertilizer: Chemical that helps plants grow.

greenhouse gases: Gases that trap the Sun's warmth in the Earth's atmosphere.

groundwater: Water that collects in cracks and pools underground.

nonpoint pollution: Pollution that does not come from a single, easy-to-find source.

landfill: Place where trash is buried.

oil slick: Large patch of oil in the water.

parasite: Animal that lives on or in another animal.

pesticide: Chemical that kills insects.

point pollution: Pollution that comes from a single, easy-to-find source.

recycle: Reuse.

Safe Drinking Water Act: Law passed in 1974 to protect U.S. drinking water from pollution.

sewage: Garbage or human waste.

thermal pollution: Changes in water temperature that harm wildlife.

water pollution: Altering water in ways that make it dangerous to use.

water treatment: A process that removes pollution from water.

wastewater: Water that has been used and is being flushed down the drain or sewage pipe.

Index

LICKDALE SCHOOL